Colour My Sketchbook

In 2014, I began uploading my sketches to Facebook.
To my delight, colourists started colouring them. It was fascinating
to see the artful interpretations of my drawings, and
this book is a celebration and continuation of that collaboration.

© Copyright 2016 Bennett Klein, all rights reserved. No part of this publication may be reproduced or distributed in any form without the written permission of the copyright owner.

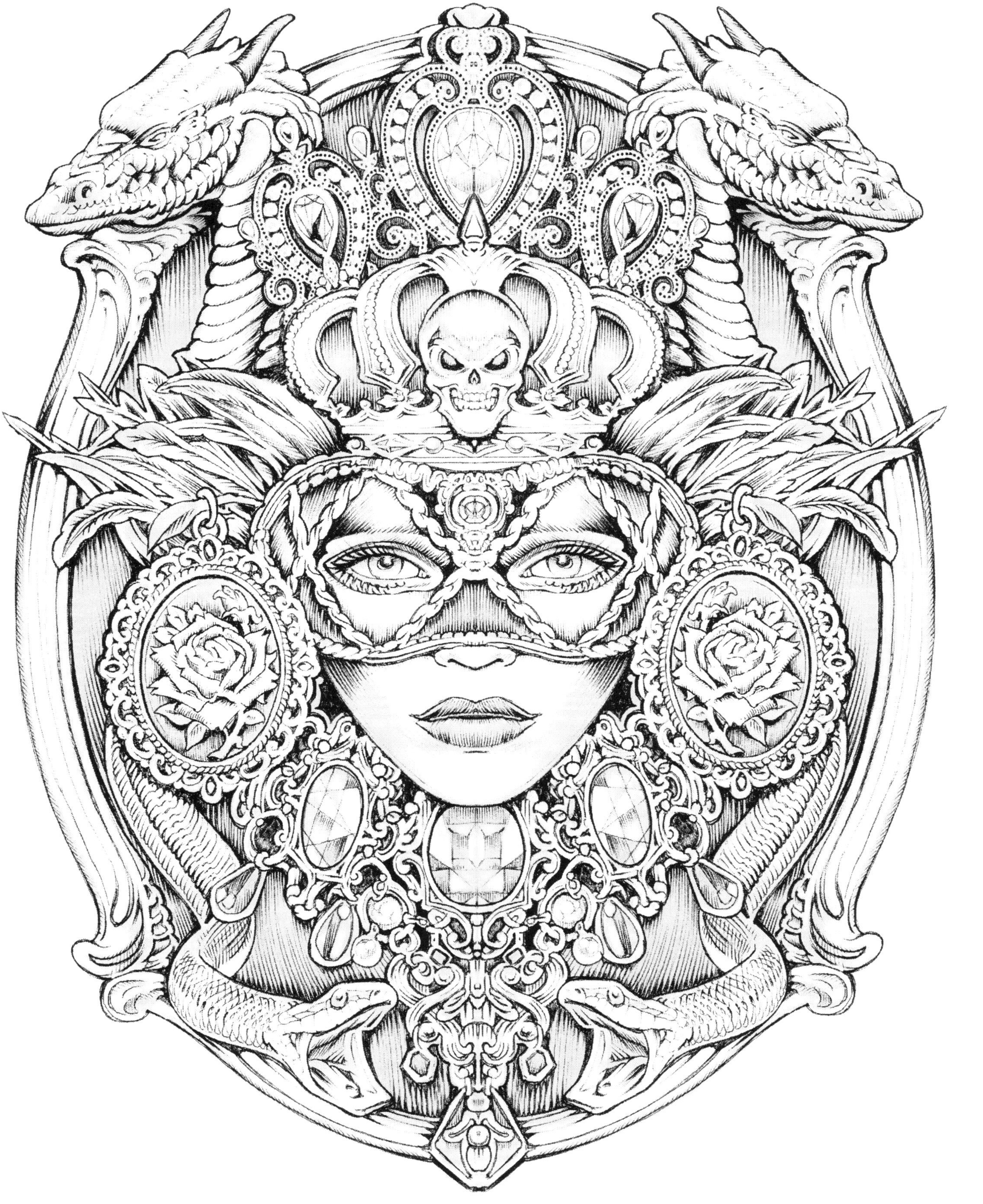

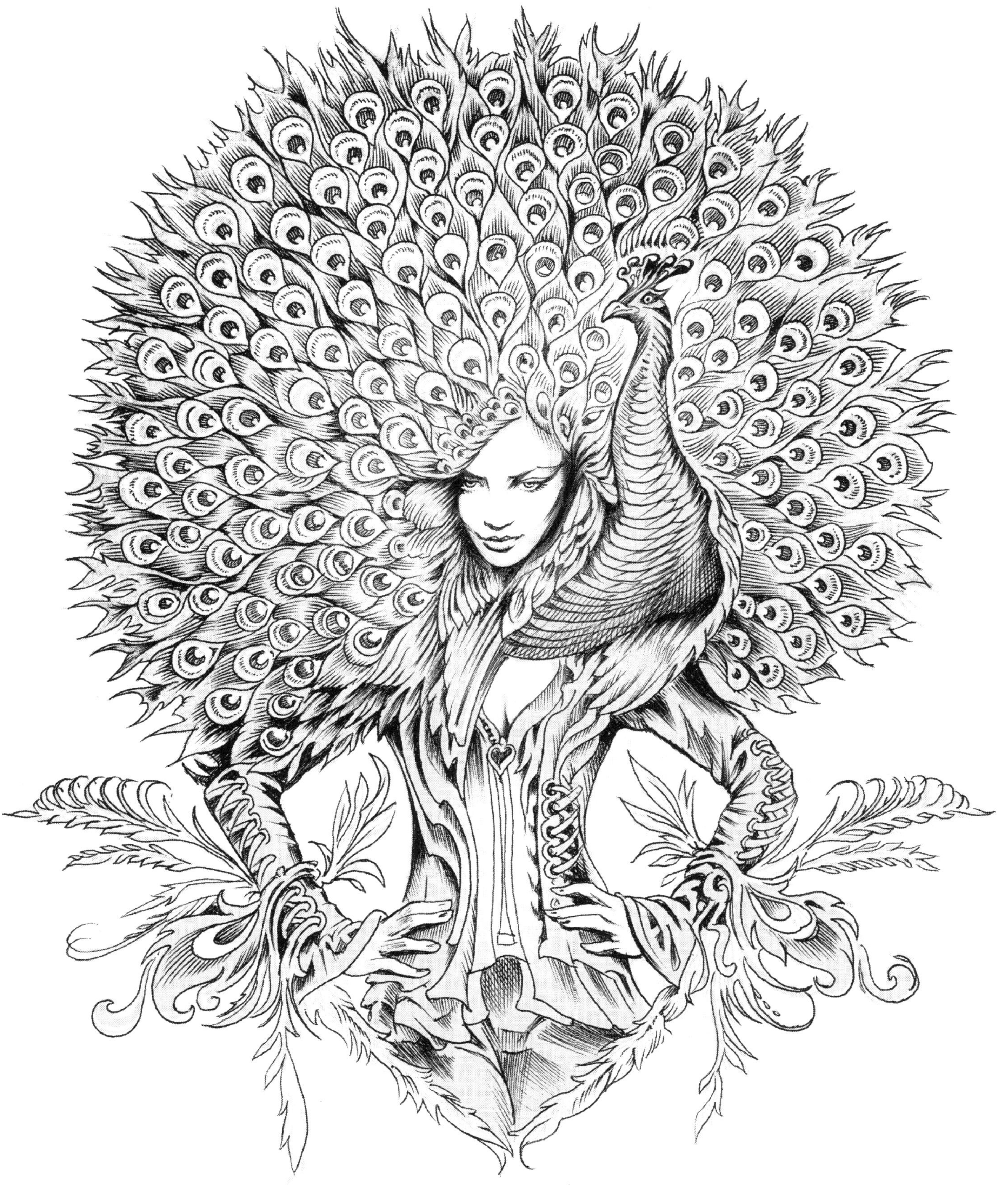

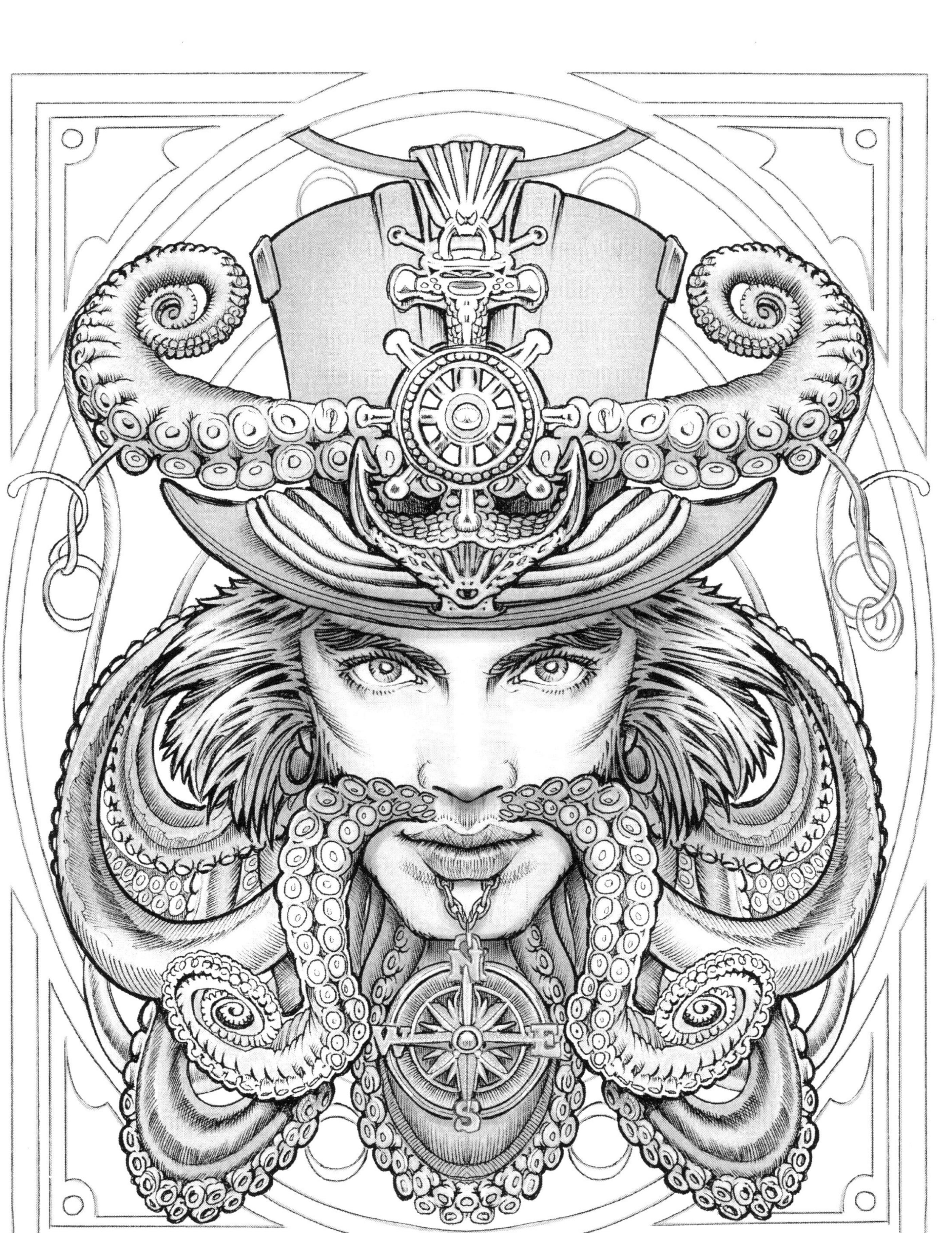
N
E
S

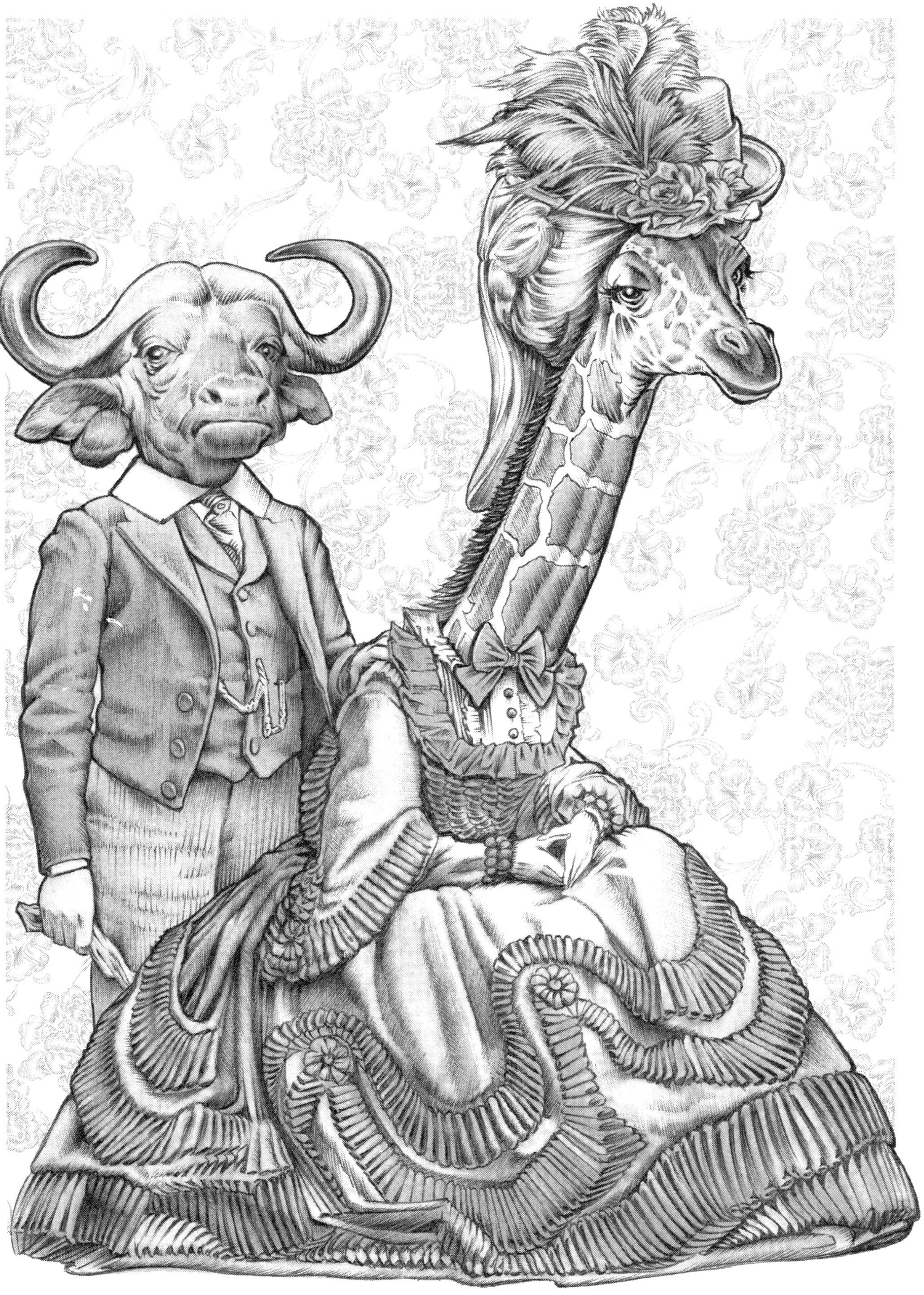

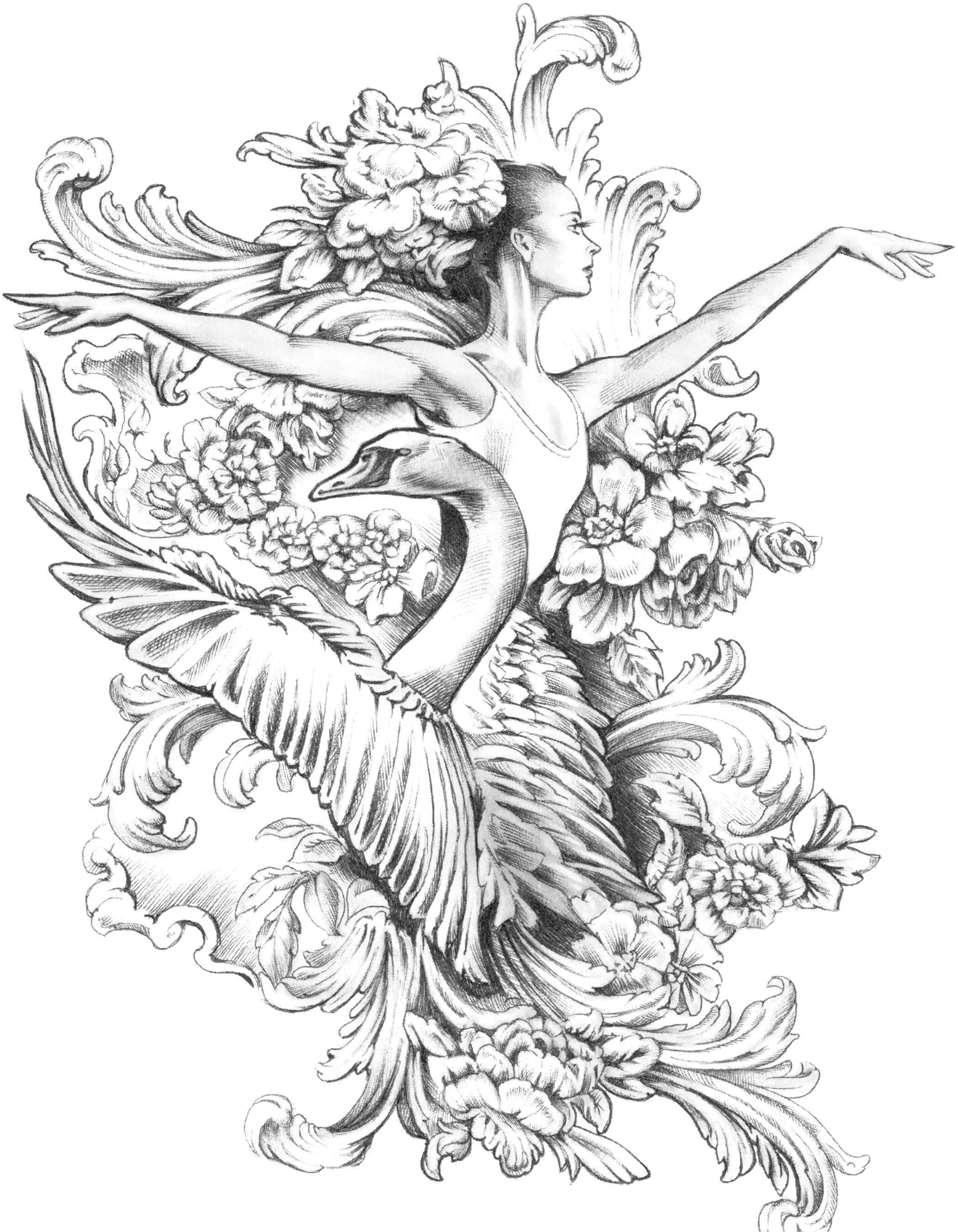

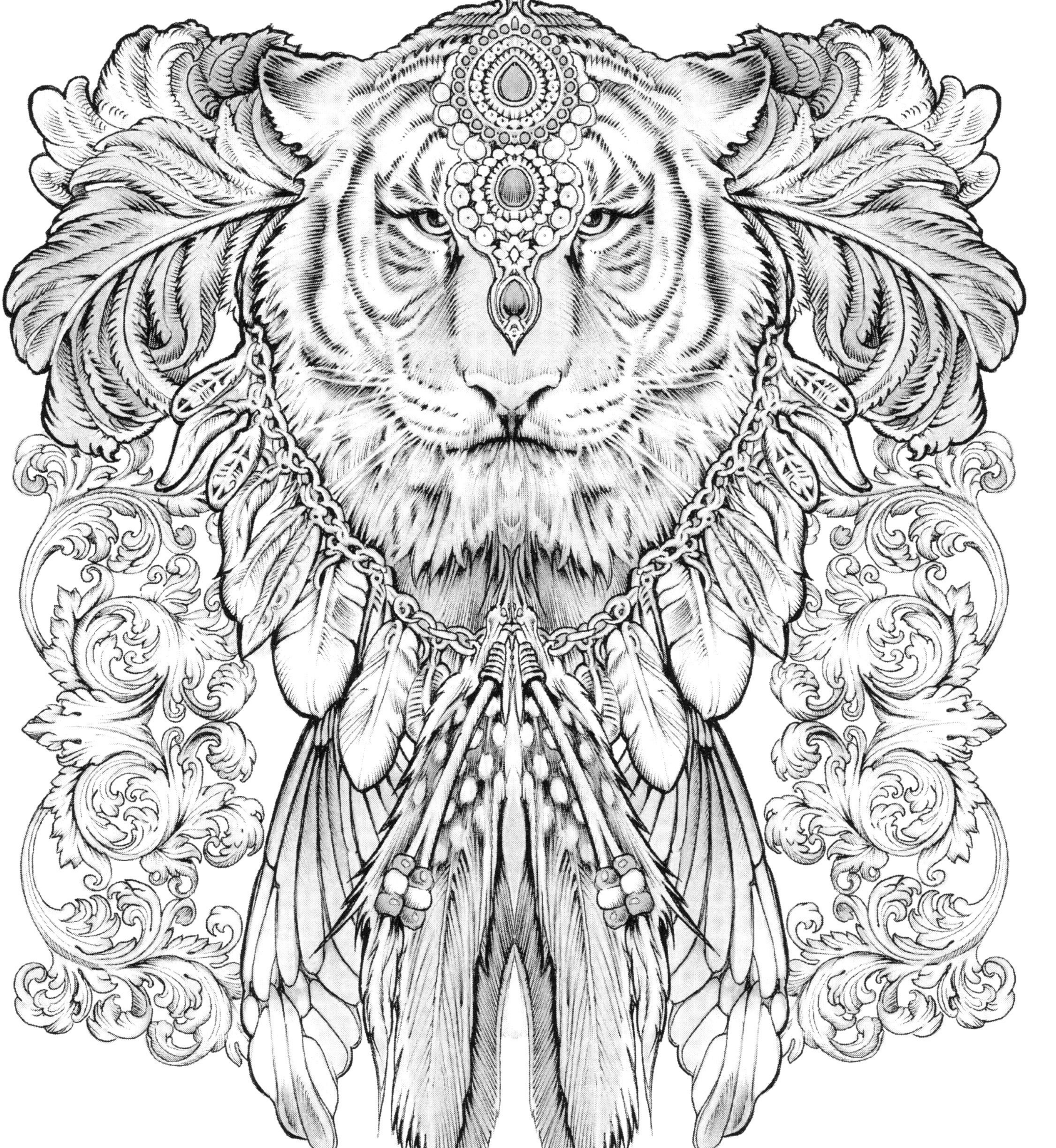

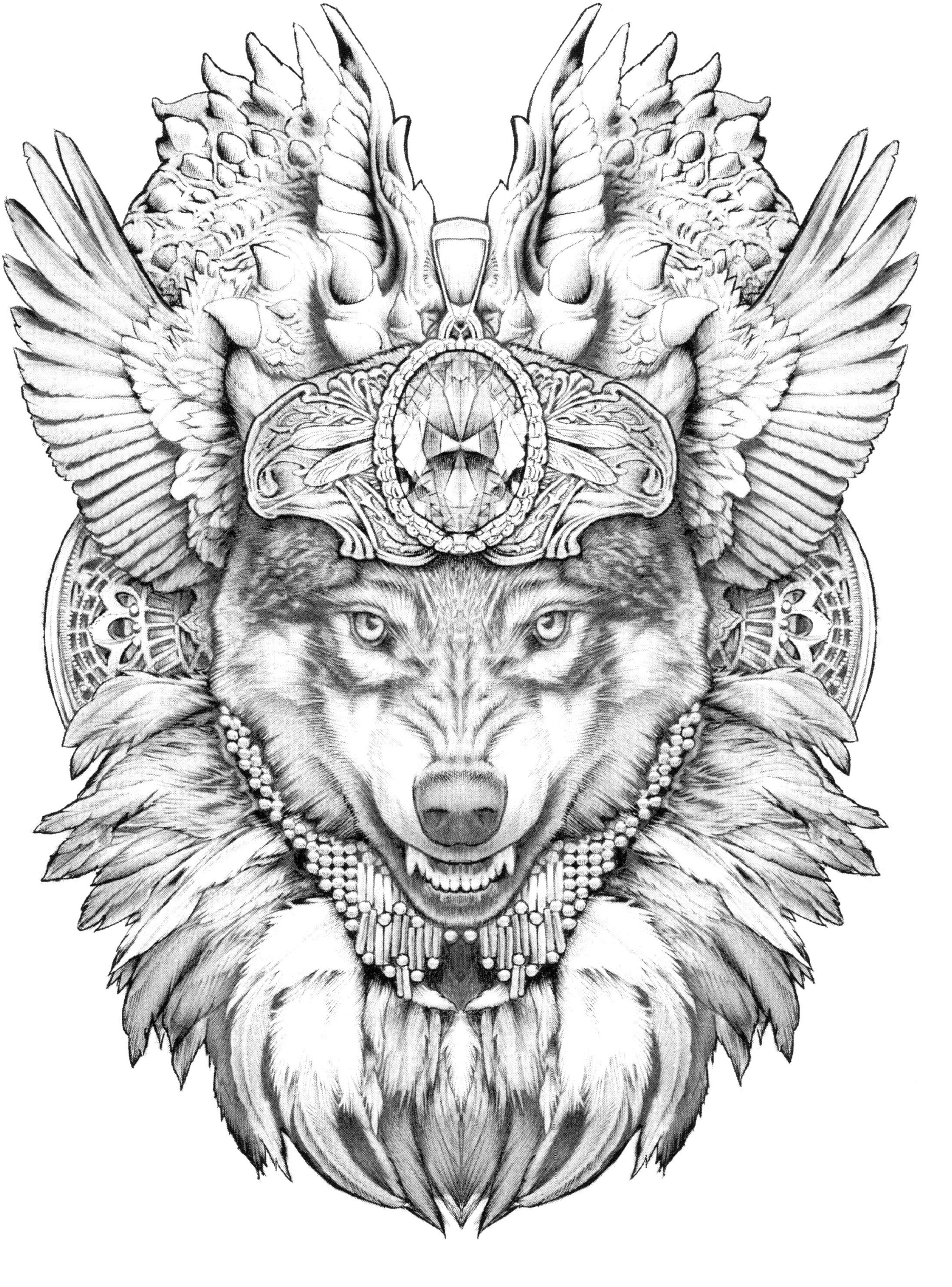

Colour My
SKETCHBOOK

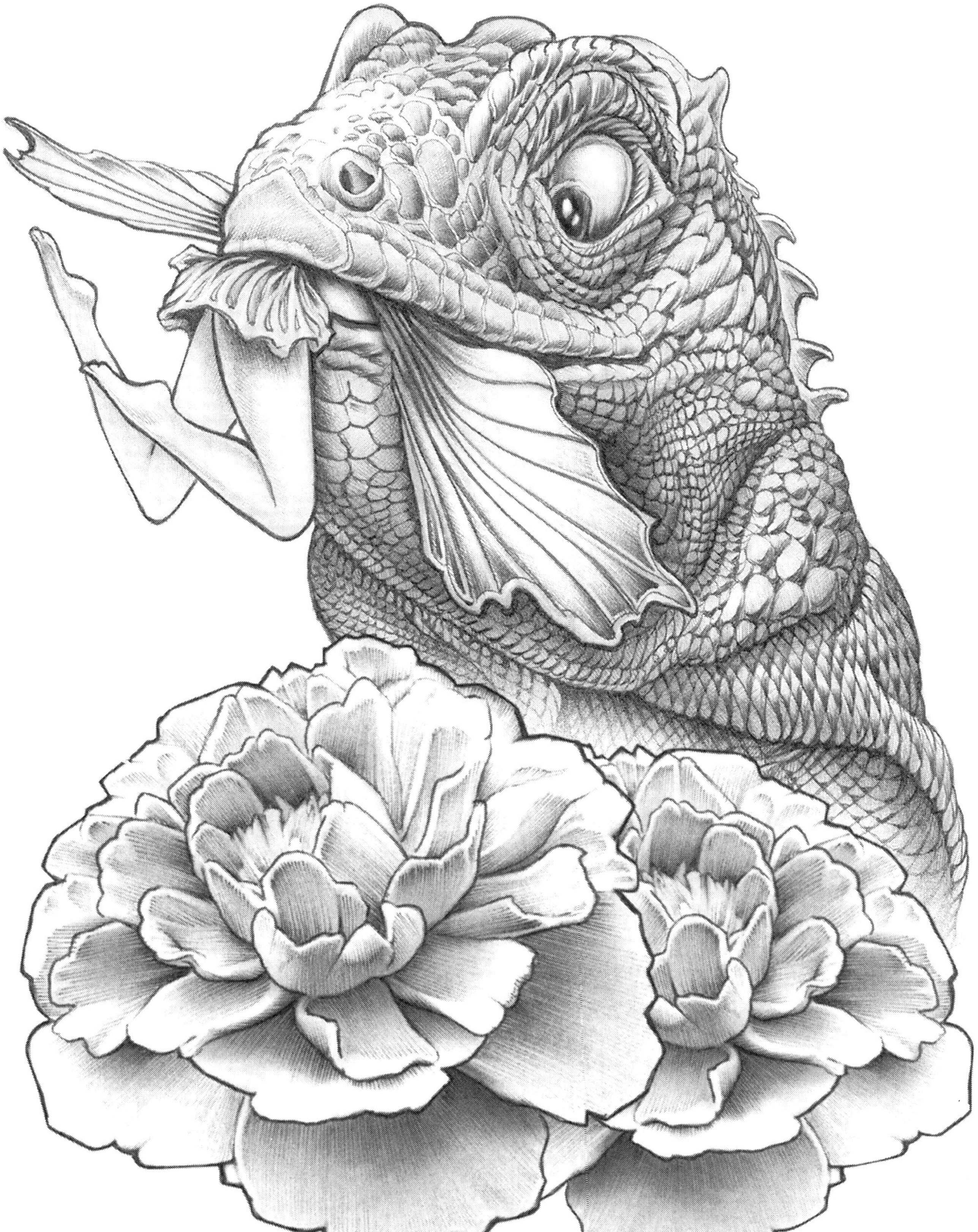

COLOUR MY
SKETCHBOOK

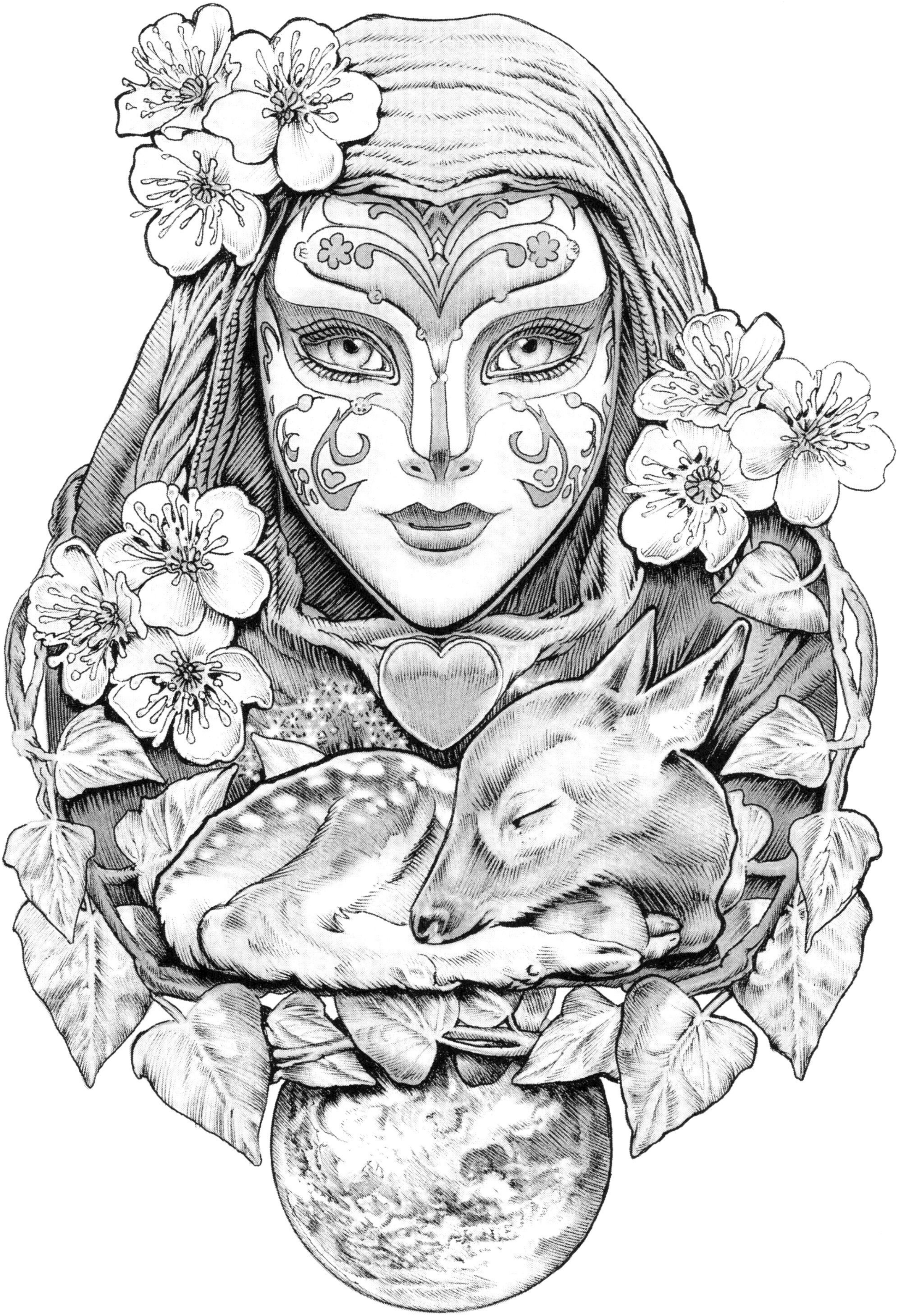

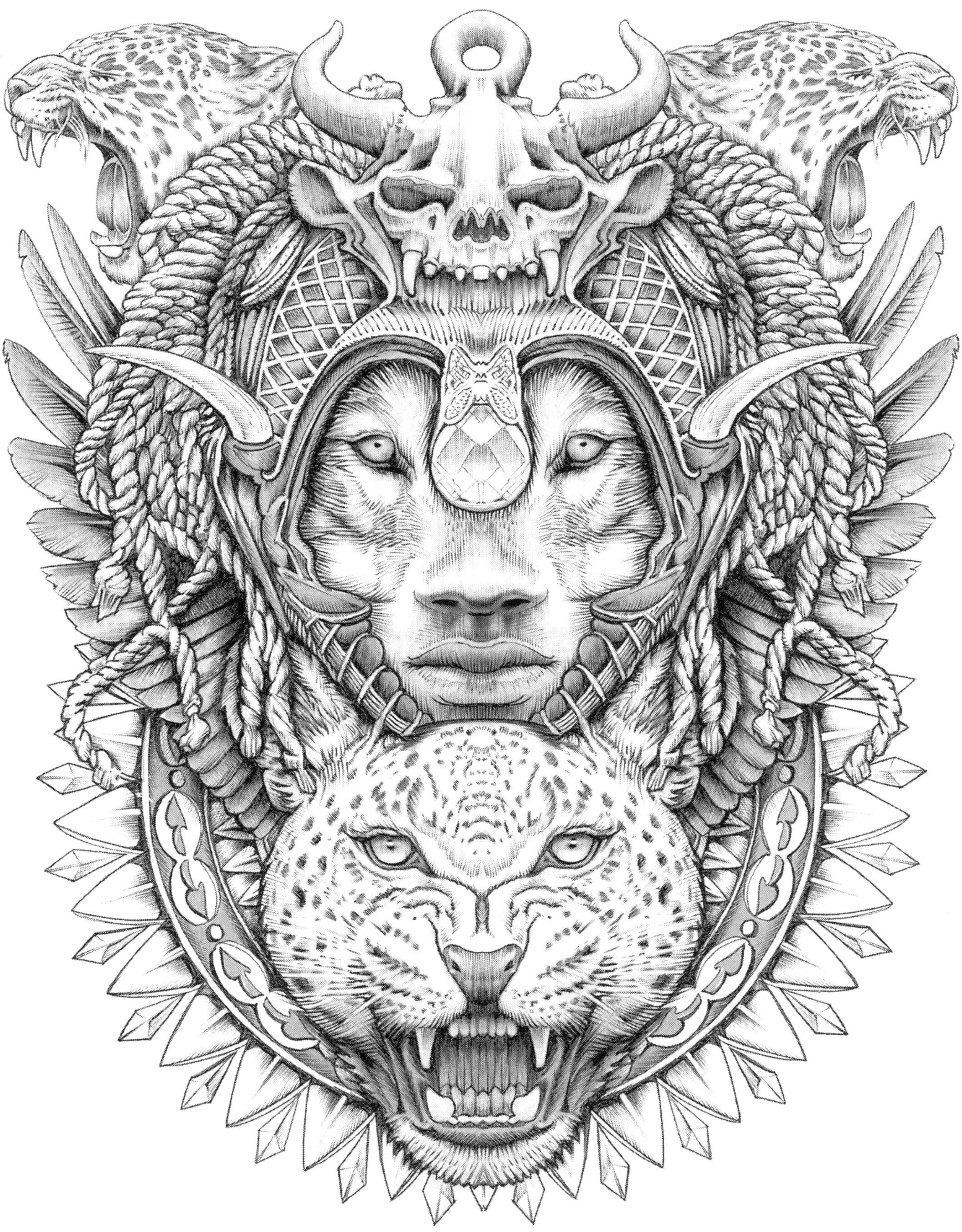

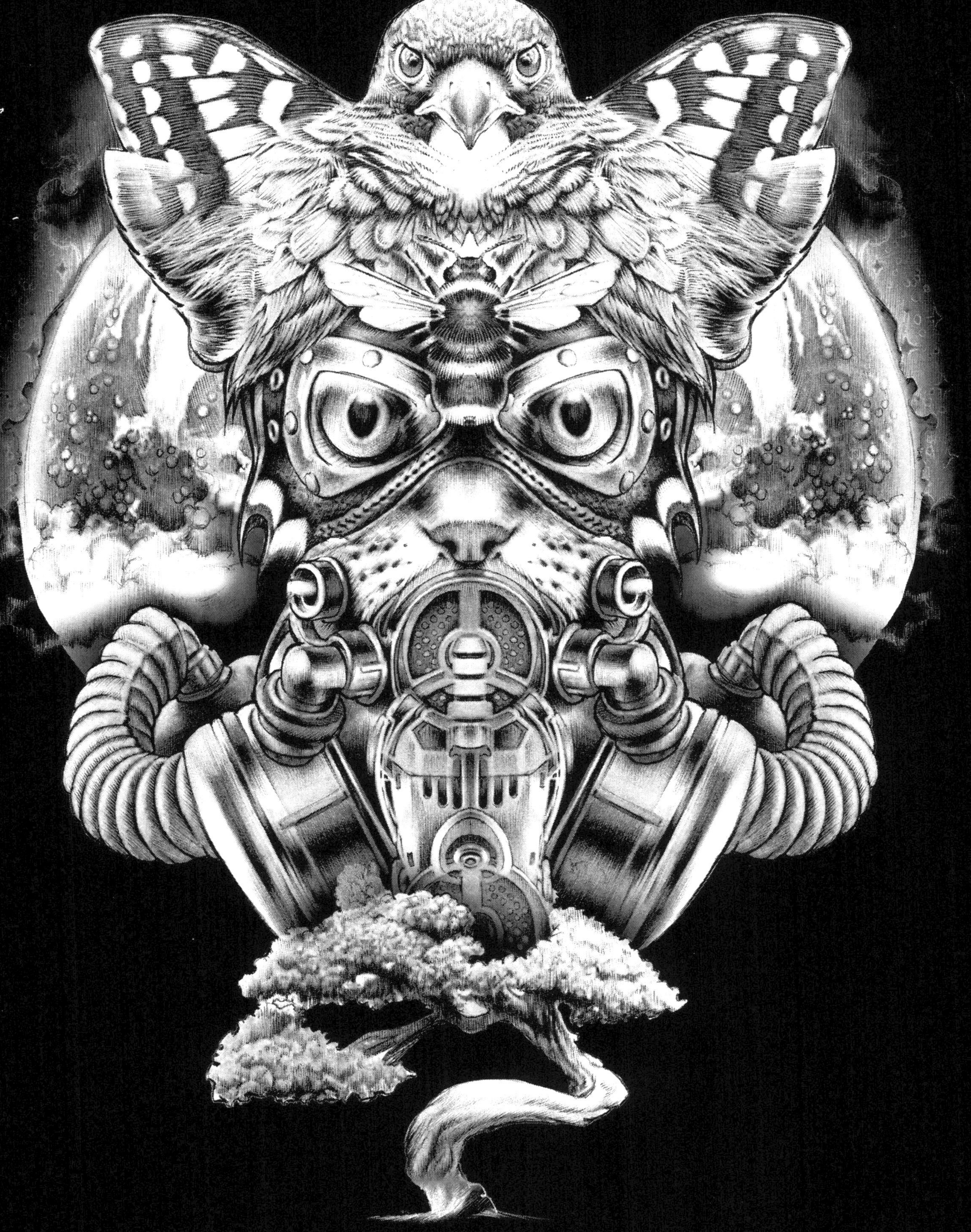

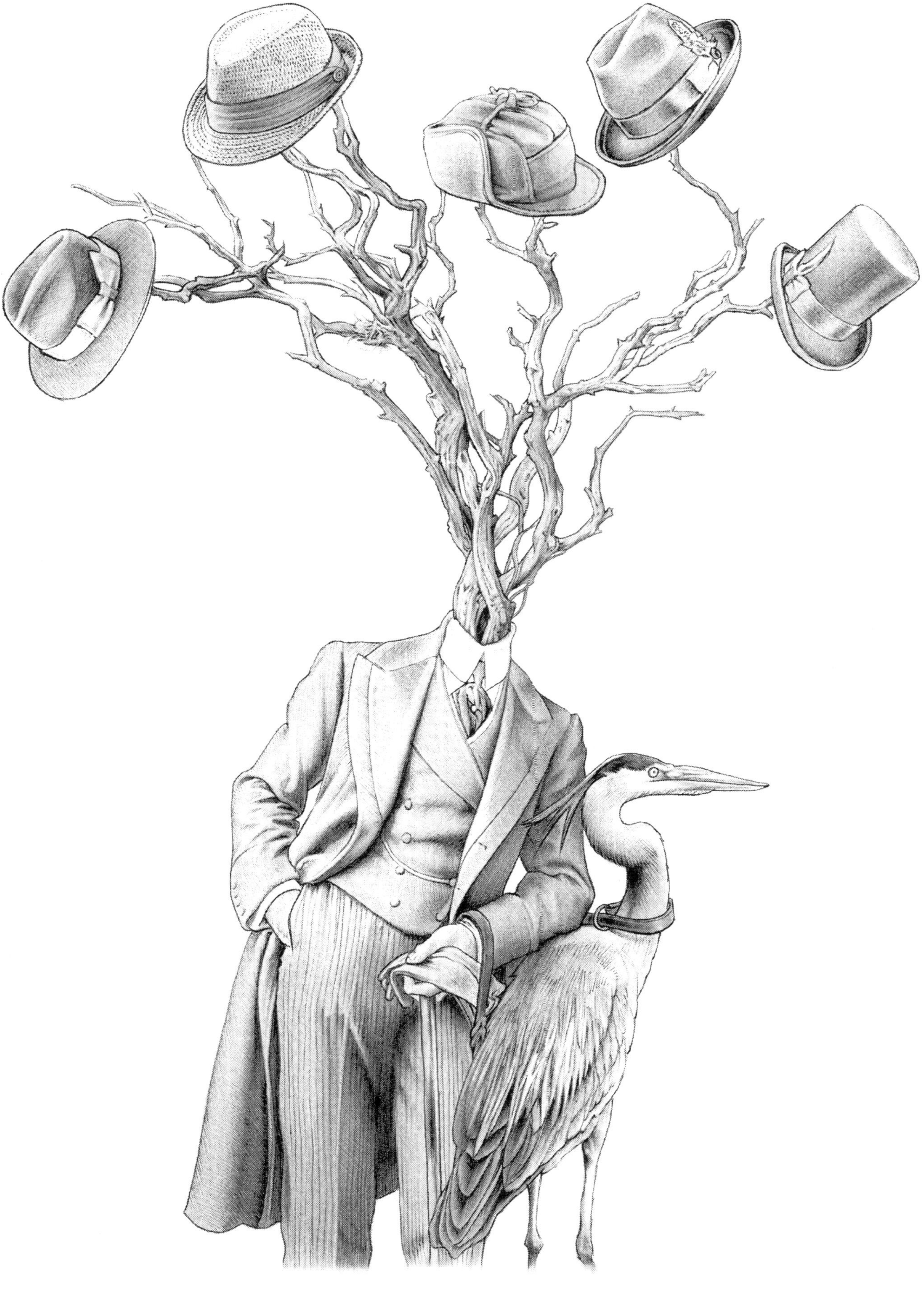

COLOUR MY
SKETCHBOOK

Thank You!

With over 30 years of professional design and illustration experience behind me, I can honestly say these books are the most creative fun I've had yet. I hope you enjoyed it too!

Printed in Great Britain
by Amazon